P9-DDY-504

"'What, me — journal?' Does the idea strike fear into over-scheduled spirituality? This is but a little book: so there's no need to be afraid of it. Still, get yourself ready for the challenge it bears.

"Margaret Smith summons the pencil to consult the heart that the paper may rejoice at our enlightenment. Smith invites us to join Frederick Buechner in that *Room Called Remember.* Her book nudges us to save the best of our pilgrimage in the sanctity of ink and paper. She does not oversell this advice by calling merely on her own experience. She enlists writers like Thoreau, Hemingway, Anne Morrow Lindbergh, Alice Walker, and Gerard Manley Hopkins. In this book you will meet a splendid gathering of literary eagles, who became eagles in penning the discourse of their hearts by staring down the scary, white pages of their journals. Afraid of this inward art? Don't be. The pencil is mightier than the terrifying secrets of your heart. Sit and write and win over your fears!"

— **CALVIN MILLER**

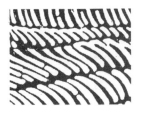

Journal Keeper

Journal Keeper

Margaret D. Smith

William B. Eerdmans Publishing Company

Grand Rapids, Michigan

Copyright © 1992 by Wm. B. Eerdmans Publishing Co.,
255 Jefferson Ave. SE, Grand Rapids, Michigan 49503
All rights reserved

Printed in the United States of America

Reprinted, June 1993

Library of Congress Cataloging-in-Publication Data

Smith, Margaret D., 1958-
    Journal keeper / Margaret D. Smith.
       p.   cm.
    ISBN 0-8028-0625-2 (pbk.)
    1. Spiritual life. 2. Diaries — Authorship — Religious aspects —
Christianity. I. Title.
BV4509.5.S635   1992
248.4'6 — dc20   92-5468
                                            CIP

The poem "Summer Grass" by Carl Sandburg originally appeared in *Good
Morning, America,* copyright © 1927, 1928, 1955, 1956 by Carl Sandburg.

For Nants

"Grace"

89374

We need never shout across the spaces to an absent God. He is nearer than our own soul, closer than our most secret thoughts.

— A. W. Tozer
The Pursuit of God

Contents

Embarking

    Your own story   3

    El Camino Real   7

    What's the difference?   9

    Begin   12

    Open form   15

    Tools   18

    Talk about the weather   21

    Surroundings   23

    Choose an event   27

    Notice things   30

Under Way

A friend   35

A name   37

Time   39

Place   42

Procrastination   45

Discipline   47

At this instant   50

He knows us   53

Pressing out   56

Why negative is normal   59

Risk   61

Find a comrade   64

Balance   67

Watchkeeping

Prayer   71

Practice the presence   74

A gentle silence   76

The mind and heart　　79

Hearing a voice　　81

Write it down　　84

Sea Journey

Look back now　　89

A pattern　　91

The parable of the pitcher　　94

Embarking

Your own story

The idea occurred to me that instead of excluding I could include all my thoughts, ideas, plans, projects, worries and concerns and make them into prayer.

— Henri J. M. Nouwen
*The Genesee Diary: Report from
a Trappist Monastery*

WHAT made you pick up this little book on journal keeping? Maybe you're the kind of book shopper who feels the urge, when passing those blank journal books, to riffle through a few, in case someone might have written in them. So far, no one ever has. But you keep looking.

Well, why don't you write in a journal book? Anyone can. As a parent you may want to record, like snapshots, both ordinary and exceptional times in your home life for your children. Or as a teenager you may want to pin down a swarm of feelings; so much is new and strange, changing every day.

As a psychology student you may have been told by the professor to keep a chronicle of your dreams. Or as a recovering hospital patient you find yourself suddenly with too much time; you can use these days to write.

If you write for a living, you might have considered carrying around a sort of sketchbook for words, raw material for later articles and books. This is a good time to start. Artists and writers use journals as seedbeds for novels, poetry, painting, sculpting, and even dance. You might want to use your journal for experimenting with words and pictures.

Or maybe you're preparing to go up into the mountains on a spiritual retreat — packing a Bible, a loaf of bread, and a thermos of coffee — and you've decided to keep a contemplative journal.

You may be a sailor of the Caribbean or an explorer of dog trails around the neighborhood. Years from now you'll want to be able to look back in your journal and remember that one sweet week in San Juan, that three-mile trek on a swampy path with your deliriously happy retriever, or perhaps that moment over coffee when your best friend pushed you to confront some painful truth about yourself, and you grew.

The point is, you want to write down your history,

your own story, as it is happening. In his book *A Room Called Remember,* Frederick Buechner sees these particular stories of ours as holy, a part of God's overarching book project. "Deep within . . . the diaries we keep," Buechner wrote, "is sacred history, is God's purpose working itself out."

No matter what reasons you might have for wanting to start a journal, consider especially this one reason: God wants to keep a journal with you. He wants to meet with us here, in our ordinary world, and in the place we usually reserve for ourselves, our hidden hearts. "In every heart there is a room," wrote the songwriter Billy Joel, "a sanctuary safe and strong." The prophet Isaiah went further, actually naming that sanctuary in the heart: "The Lord Almighty is the one you are to regard as holy. He will be a sanctuary."

One early evening a friend of mine and I took a drive to St. Edward's State Park on Lake Washington. We were talking about the Lakota Indian Black Elk's prayer: "Grandfather, you have made the hard road and the good road to cross, and where they meet is a holy place." At the park we sat in the curve of a doorway on the stone steps of an empty seminary and wrote in our journals. The swallows shuttled from grass to roof, twittering as they do, but everything else was silent. When we looked up from our writing, we both smiled and said together, "This is a holy place!" God is a sanctuary like that park. We can open our journals in his presence and be with him there.

You may think of your journal as a dumping ground

for worries, a junkyard for observations that no one else would care to read. But when you address your journal to God, everything in it is turned into prayer. Whatever you decide to write in your journal can be written to God. Write to him about the bad wheat crop this year, the mediocre sermon you just heard, the great watercolor painting you saw at today's sidewalk art sale. If you agree that everything you write to God is prayer, then let go of the idea that some things aren't quite spiritual enough to include here.

Nothing is too ordinary to write about. The word *ordinary* comes from the word *order*. When you write in your journal about the ordinary, you are making order out of a jumble of thoughts. Soon you will notice a pattern developing. Events and thoughts that may have seemed random or mundane begin to piece themselves together in a mosaic pattern. The shape of your life becomes easier to see when it's set down on paper.

When you are honestly ready to start keeping a journal, all you need is a nudge. I hope this book is the nudge you need.

The readers will find in my diary a random collection of what I have seen on the road, views somehow remaining in my heart.

— Bashō
Narrow Road to the Deep North

El Camino Real

We knew God as a listening God who had waited a long time to be in conversation with us.

— Elizabeth O'Connor
Journey Inward, Journey Outward

SPANISH missions in California are spaced a day's walk apart. All along El Camino Real, "The King's Highway," early missionaries could walk for a day, then stop at the next mission for food, conversation, prayer, and rest.

Your journal book is like those Spanish missions. Every page is a stopping point after a day's travels, a place to refresh you, then send you on your way. Your journal is a place to be quiet, to reflect and commune with God. Imagine meeting Jesus at a mission. He invites you to sit down, relax, and tell him about the day's journey. Imagine him leaning toward you, smiling as you talk with him. At times he reassures you, and at other times he startles you with bracing words.

So they drew near to the village to which they were going. [Jesus] appeared to be going further, but they constrained him, saying, "Stay with us, for it is toward evening and the day is now far spent." So he went in to stay with them. . . . [Later] they said to each other, "Did not our hearts burn within us while he talked to us?"

— Luke 24:28-29, 32 (RSV)

What's the difference?

"Eh? Two views? There are a dozen views about everything, until you know the answer. Then there's never
more than one. But it's no affair of mine."

— character of Hingest in C. S. Lewis's
That Hideous Strength

WHAT do you want to call your record of thoughts:
a diary or a journal? The words *diary* and *journal*
both come from the same Indo-European root *deiw*, meaning "daily; to shine," from which we also get the words
deity, journey, sky, jovial, dismal, and *Tuesday,* by the way.

Is there a difference between a diary and a journal?
I don't think so. The definitions seem interchangeable,
according to one's whim. Some see a diary as a place to
record one's most intimate dreams and most searing

insights. They see a journal, on the other hand, as a place to record events like "Cat died. Put the corn in; weather hot." Others reverse those definitions.

I call mine a journal, because to my ear it sounds more grown up than a diary. In third grade I was given a One Year Diary with the date on every page, lines too narrow for expansive thought, and a peacock on the latched cover. A sample entry from those days: "We went to Carmel. Our motel was the Green Lantern. We had dinner at the Clambox."

But now I remember why I wrote that entry. Even at age eight I was in love with intriguing words, and I liked to taste them on my tongue. *Carmel, Green Lantern, Clambox.*

Years ago, rugged men like Davy Crockett kept diaries, which I am quite sure did not sport peacocks on the covers. But diaries seem to have slipped out of fashion, especially for adults. Why do people now attend "journal" workshops instead of "diary" workshops? I think the word *journal* implies, at least these days, serious and essential stuff.

Some friends of mine keep what they call a prayer journal or a spiritual journal. These are good terms for the book you will be keeping, as long as the terms don't limit what you want to write inside.

But call your book what you will. Personal preference is the rule, in this case. Ralph Waldo Emerson and Anne Morrow Lindbergh called their daily writings diaries. A contemporary pianist named Carol Mont Parker wrote a "chronicle" of the six months leading up to her debut at Carnegie Recital Hall. Mary Ann Lynch toys with our notions of a normal journal, using pictures as well as words in her book entitled *Combinations: A Journal of Photography*. And in seventeenth-century Japan, the poet Bashō modestly referred to his finely etched entries as "travel sketches."

As of today I have decided to keep a diary again — just a place where I can write my thoughts and opinions when I have a moment. Somehow I have to keep and hold the rapture of being seventeen.

— Sylvia Plath, poet
Diary entry

Begin

All writing is communication.

— E. B. White, essayist

THE most common question that new journal keepers ask is, How do you start? That's easy. As my mother's word-thrifty grandmother used to say when she picked up the telephone, "Begin."

Never mind about all the blank white space on the page; you fill it gradually, a few words at a time. Write as though you were talking on the phone with a friend. "Hi," you might begin. "I bought a journal book today at the bookstore café on Seventh Avenue. At first I wasn't planning to buy anything but a cappuccino, but then I accidentally bought this, too."

Using a large artist's sketchbook and a calligraphy

pen, I started my own journal in earnest on August 11, 1983, just after attending Colonel Heath "Bo" Bottomly's journal workshop in Seattle. This is my first entry:

> To be a writer I need to practice writing and some fine day I will be as proficient in calligraphy as in procrastination. The day is dark and wet, like Petersburg in October. I am so filled with new fresh talk on words I sit shaking my head with bubbles inside. Maybe I've been sitting on a shelf for a year and God said, "I'm going to use you now" and shook well. Now to apply. Bo Bottomly said to record feelings in a journal every day. Today I feel thankful for all these writers who speak the same sweet language.

Just as you knew how to sing when you were two, and no one had to teach you how to play in the snow, you already know how to begin a journal: just start writing. If you've tried before to keep one but could never find a place to write, then here's the place, right in this book — in the margins and in the other places that have been left open for you.

And if you always wanted to write down your thoughts but could never find a way to justify the time, this book will help you set aside time to begin a journal. More importantly, it will spur you to keep on writing in it, after the first glow has worn off.

Here, you can write your journal entry to God and listen for his words to you. This kind of writing is visible prayer. It's communication but it's more than communication: it's communion, a friendship deepened through quiet conversation.

Use this book as you begin writing your journal. If you've already started your own journal, use the book as a support and an incentive to keep writing every day. This is a scrapbook of quotes and thoughts, with space that invites you to record your own ideas and experiences. Think of the book as a friend's daily notes to you, asking, "How are you doing? Are you still writing?"

Make a promise here to write an entry every day, at least until you fill up your *Journal Keeper.*

Signed _____

Date _____

The idea is to get the pencil moving quickly.

— Bernard Malamud, novelist

Open form

June 20, 1942. It's an odd idea for someone like me to keep a diary; not only because I have never done so before, but because it seems to me that neither I — nor for that matter anyone else — will be interested in the unbosomings of a thirteen-year-old schoolgirl.

> — Anne Frank
> *Anne Frank: The Diary*
> *of a Young Girl*

YOU may never know how important your journal will become. Since your journal is a record of days, you should follow some sort of form to help you arrange your thoughts and to create a pattern you can recognize. No matter how you have — or have not — kept a journal in the past, try this open form, at least for a week or so.

Write your first entry here. And instead of writing to yourself, write it as a letter to God, as Alice Walker's character Celie did in *The Color Purple:*

> Dear God,
>   Sofia would make a dog laugh, talking about those people she work for. They have the nerve to try to make us think slavery fell through because of us, say Sofia. Like us didn't have sense enough to handle it.

Date _____

Town _____

Time _____

Place (desk, beach . . .) _____

Talk about the weather.

Describe your surroundings.

Tell about one event of the day that bothered you, amused you, or otherwise caught your attention.

Offer a reaction, a question, a song, a poem snatch,

a problem, a sketch, a quote, a letter, overheard conversation. Anything that comes to mind or heart. A photograph, a newspaper clipping. A leaf.

Listen.

USE this form as long as you want to, letting your ideas flow onto the blank parts of this book if you like. Your words might begin to spill from this book into a blank book or into a word processor. As you continue to write, you may find the form changing. Good! Your journal will gradually shape itself to the way you've always wanted to write, the way your heart wants to speak.

There's no rule on how it is to write. Sometimes it comes easily and perfectly. Sometimes it is like drilling rock and then blasting it out with charges.

— Ernest Hemingway
Selected Letters

Tools

The journal was typed out, slapdash, as fast as my fingers would allow.

— Maxine Kumin, poet

THE tools of this trade could not be simpler. All you need is paper and a pen, or variations. To begin, you don't even need paper. Keep writing your entries here in this book between the quotes and encouragements, wherever you find the space.

Experiment with all your different writing instruments, from ballpoints to colorful marker pens. My friend Rose, who is an English professor and poet, likes a green pen; it makes her think of growing things, and that helps her to feel creative. Amy, another friend and a longtime journal keeper, writes with a fountain pen, having grown accustomed to using fountain pens at school in Holland.

When you find a writing tool that fits you, keep using it, to give a little order to your journal life. But don't be afraid to change as your needs and preferences change. When I first started my journal I wrote brief, careful entries, using a calligraphy pen with a thick nib. Now I scribble four or five pages a night, heedless of penmanship, writing with a black rolling-tip pen that's fast and fun.

When your writings start to spill out of this book, what other tools will you use? Of course, you could use a typewriter, as Maxine Kumin did, if you don't mind the keys clacking while you're trying to contemplate. A neighbor of mine writes her journal entries on a word processor every night. She keeps volumes of journals on disks and even has a data base for cross-referencing. She has the most efficient system of journal keeping I have ever heard of. But she says she misses the beautifully bound journal books her mother had given her every year since she was nine.

I do like the ease of a word processor for other kinds of writing, but for my journal I still use those blank books you see in gift stores and bookstores. Blank books are so quiet that if you put your ear to them, you can almost hear the ocean. Set side by side, their covers make a mosaic, and their pages invite you to sprawl, scrawl, sketch, and press friends' notes inside.

Find a style of journal that fits you comfortably, like a corduroy bathrobe you wear every night. If the robe wears out, buy another one that suits you now. But keep the old robe in a drawer. Every now and then, hold it up to yourself and look in a mirror.

Jan. 1, 1978. This diary looked so inviting when I first bought it. But this isn't big enough, for one thing; I feel limited by the short page. And it doesn't open up, bend nicely, invite me to write, like the first hole of a good golf course should invite you to play.

— Susan Kinnicutt, writer
Diary entry

Talk about the weather

"I can't think of anything to write."

WHEN faced with an awkward silence after polite introductions, I always feel a bit terrified. Maybe you feel the same way when approached by a blank journal page. To get past the awkward stage, start your entry as you begin a conversation, with a comment on the weather. How you choose to talk or write about the weather is a subtle way of telling how you feel at the time. In 1855, Henry David Thoreau wrote, "In a journal it is important in a few words to describe the weather, or character of the day, as it affects our feelings. That which was so important at the time cannot be unimportant to remember."

Look out the window and describe the sky, the rain,

or the color of the clouds today. I've heard that a certain tribe of Native Americans in Alaska has twenty words for "snow." A little boy I met in rainy southeast Alaska made up a new term for precipitation. He saw the mist outside and described it to me as "kind of a dry rain."

Say it simply, in shorthand: "Fog settles in low places" or "Steel-blue skies." Or say it in a slightly more complex way, as poet May Sarton described a January cold snap in her book entitled *Journal of a Solitude:* "A little warmer this morning, zero instead of twenty below. With an extra blanket over the electric blanket I slept in warmth, less shivery around the edges than the night before. I slept and woke and thought about this journal."

The small act of describing the wind and other weather can reveal your state of mind and heart.

A sweet summer afternoon. Cool breezes and a clean sky. This day will not come again.

— Thomas Merton, contemplative
Diary entry

Surroundings

Two days ago [I was] out petting some horses and feeding them grass from places they couldn't reach. I can still smell that fresh horse smell, a combination of earth, herbs, dry grass. They smell like autumn, old rotting apples.

— Linda Hogan, writer
Diary entry

AS you give an account of the place where you are writing, use all your senses. Whether you write in a park or in a crowded train traveling cross-country, you are bound to be, naturally, surrounded by your surroundings. Look around; find an object of interest. If you are sitting in a park, describe how the swallows are flying. Are they dip-swinging or fluttering in place at their nest? Now close your mouth and eyes and take a deep breath.

Why does that smell of cologne wafting over from the neighboring park bench seem so familiar? The poet Gerard Manley Hopkins noticed everything on his walks, even the location of smells:

> July 12, 1874. I noticed the smell of the big cedar, not just in passing it but always in a patch of sunlight on the walk a little way off. I found the bark smelt in the sun and not in the shade and I fancied too this held even of the smell it shed in the air.

When you take your journal outside, listen to all the sounds, then pick out a particular sound to write about. One fall morning I sat out in a gazebo on Governors Island and wrote this entry in my journal:

> A bell buoy clangs in New York Harbor like a church bell calling. It has two tones, not *ding* and *dong* but two ways of saying the same thing, one high tone, one a little lower. A one-word question and an answer, the same word: Yes? Yes. The question asked over and over, and a patient answer, the same one.

Don't forget to use the senses that are hard to capture in words: taste and touch. Contrary to what you might have learned in school, it's all right to describe one sense in terms of another. Your English teacher knew the concept as synesthesia. When you wrote in a class assignment, "The corned beef tasted like a rusty bridge," your teacher either praised your ingenuity or marked it with "Does this make sense???" "Yes," you might have said quietly. "To me it does." It made sense to you because, in some peculiar way, it was true. In your journal, put no limits on your imagination. You can describe the clear night sky as salty with stars, or an old man's voice as dusty.

Why should it matter that you capture the senses when writing in your private journal? Because you will look back on your entry years from now. When you succeed in catching in words a trip to the circus by describing the sights and sounds and smells of it, you will be able to see it again. You will even remember details you did not write down: the boy behind you kept kicking the back of your seat, your friend bought you a pinwheel that glittered when it spun, and you felt sympathy for the tigers!

You can create sparks in your writing by banging words together like chunks of flint. Listen to young children, who love to say anything that comes to mind. To describe what they don't know, they use small, bright words they *do* know. When our older son J. B. was three, he liked running around the yard in "just feet." At two, his brother Eric watched the trees waving in the wind and asked, "Why do the trees say bye?" When you write down small, bright words in your journal, your entries become clear and strong and memorable.

*1933. I sit at the desk and look out at the dark cedars;
my feet get cold in spite of the gas fire. . . . It feels like
college. Charles is away and I alone. The little room, the
rain, the Sunday feeling, the cramp at the desk, the work
hanging over you and Yorkshire pudding for lunch.*

— Anne Morrow Lindbergh, writer
Diary entry

Choose an event

Sept. 3, 1787. Visited a Machine at Doctr. Franklin's (called a Mangle) for pressing, in place of ironing, clothes from the Wash. Which Machine is well calculated for Table cloths and such articles as have not pleats and irregular foldings. . . .

— George Washington
Diary entry

CHOOSE one event of the day, one episode that made an impression, rather than listing all the happenings of the day. Any episode from your day, even if it's a conversation you held with the bank teller, can be charming.

Focusing on one event is like training your camera on a particular object, such as a bright starfish at low tide in Monterey Bay. Instead of using a wide-angle lens to encompass a whole beach in one snapshot, come back again tomorrow and the next day, taking a different detail picture each time. When my family and I lived on the Oregon Coast I often wrote in my journal about people at the beach:

> Strolling through tourists with Bonnie in Cannon Beach today. Bonnie said, "I don't look at the tourists — they're like the tide that goes in and out, and the natives are like the treasures that are left behind in the little coves."

Choose something trifling, if you like. What may seem at first dull or insignificant in The Great Scheme of Things often brightens and gains importance when it's written down. Suppose you attended a wedding today. You might feel that you *should* write something about the bride, the groom, the attendants, and the important guests. But at the reception was an old man with a long white beard and bird-blue eyes, and he smiled as he bent to tie a little boy's shoe. You could write about that. Centuries ago the Japanese poet Bashō recorded this in his journal:

> Shortly before daybreak, the moon began to shine through the rifts made in the hanging clouds. I immediately wakened the priest, and other members of the household followed him out of bed. We sat for a long time in utter silence, watching the moonlight trying to penetrate the clouds and listening to the sound of the lingering rain.

Well-chosen details of the most ordinary situation can turn it into a crisp and graceful story.

Outside my window the song sparrow is singing loudly. For him it is not yet time to go to bed. It is seven o'clock and still very light. But I had better stop if I want to sing at 2 A.M. when the song sparrow sleeps.

— Henri J. M. Nouwen,
contemplative

Notice things

1954. Looking into the journal I kept during the 1933 European journey — I see how, at the time, the power of seeing and hearing and noting down had developed. The diary kept in Vienna in 1922 was without any real descriptive power. . . . Even at 24 I noticed practically nothing.

— Louise Bogan, poet
Journal entry

AFTER taking note of your surroundings, really *notice* them. The word *notice* literally means "to begin to be acquainted with." As a journal keeper who might write down anything at all today, you have the happy duty of making the acquaintance of all sorts of curiosities of God's and people's design: a girl's face and a lighthouse, a peony and a faded blue shirt.

When you take a walk in a sculpture garden or meet a certain child for the first time, look! Take note of detail, as painters do. The Dutch Impressionist painter Vincent Van Gogh wrote reams of description to his brother Theo. In one letter he wrote,

> On Sunday if you had been with us you would have seen a red vineyard, all red like red wine. In the distance it turned to yellow, and then a green sky with the sun, the earth after the rain violet, sparkling yellow here and there where it caught the reflection of the setting sun.

Catching vibrant colors in writing must have strengthened Van Gogh's later paintings of scenes like this. Such loving detail in both his writing and his art came from intense and patient observation.

Paying close attention won't disturb your sense of wonder; it will deepen your sense of praise. Gerard Manley Hopkins took painstaking notes on works of God ranging from the Northern Lights to pigeons. After scrutinizing the waves at the Isle of Man in 1872, he wrote in his journal,

> Looked at to the right or left they are scrolled over like mouldboards or feathers or jibsails seen by the edge. It is pretty to see the hollow of the barrel disappearing as the white comb on each side runs along the wave gaining

ground till the two meet at a pitch and crush and overlap each other.

Hopkins might have used this journal entry later to write the following lines in his poem called "Henry Purcell":

The thunder-purple seabeach, plumed purple-of-thunder,
. . . his palmy snow-pinions scatter a colossal smile.

Like Anne Frank, her neighbor in Holland, Etty Hillesum died young in a concentration camp, having left behind only a soulful diary. Hillesum, whose diary entries were collected in *An Interrupted Life,* had hoped to become a writer. A few years before her death, she made an entry in her diary about the power of writing down the particulars:

Looked at Japanese prints this afternoon. That's how I want to write. Attention to the smallest detail — and all around it space, not empty but inspired.

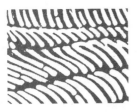

Under Way

A friend

April 1, 1791. I wove two yards and three quarters and three inches to-day and I think I did pretty well considering it was April Fool Day.

— Elizabeth Fuller,
American settler's child
Diary entry

BY keeping a journal every day, you develop a kind of happy friendship with it. You can tell it jokes and ask it questions. You keep it filled; it keeps you warmed. And in a way, it answers you, agreeing with your thoughts. "A diary means 'yes indeed,'" said the poet Gertrude Stein.

When you write your journal entries to God, you swing to an even wider circle of friendship. You and God now deepen your friendship through prayer in the journal. Once I wrote in my journal,

Knowing God is like knowing a friend. Little by little as you spend time with him and find out all the intricacies you can, you love him more and share and spend yourself with him.

This relationship is a living thing. Though it's rooted, it's not static. It whirls around like a sea anemone when the tide comes in.

An old woman of the mountains of Guatemala used to visit a missionary woman in the village. Before the old woman left the missionary's house, she would bow and pay her hostess the greatest compliment: "I will come again, for I like myself when I am with you." If you like yourself when you are writing in your journal, you will feel more and more at home there. As an old saying goes, "Friendship is where two hearts can meet and be at home." Your journal is that home where you and God can meet, again and again.

You and I are what we are when we are alone [with Jesus]. Talk with Him, listen to Him, look at Him.

— Corrie ten Boom, Holocaust survivor
This New Day

A name

To be named is to be known.

— Nancy Iremonger, playwright

IT'S always nice to name the things you love. By naming something, you begin to know it more intimately. When Ralph Waldo Emerson was a teenager, he named the early volumes of his diary. "I love my 'Wide Worlds,'" he wrote in one entry. I remember that as a camper in North Carolina I would watch a counselor scribbling down his impressions of the campfire meetings in a journal he had titled "Black Book."

All authors name their books, so it's puzzling that not many journal keepers name their journals. If you name your journal, it will be like naming a child. Call your journal whatever you would like it to become: Shade Tree, Radical, Long Song, Parachute.

I found the name for my journal at a church business meeting. The church treasurer had labeled his account ledger, in large block letters, "FRONT." Did it mean FRONT cover? FRONT as a cover for unethical activities? Storm FRONT? Russian FRONT? The title looked so important, and at the same time so silly, I felt I had to steal it. With a name like "FRONT, vol. 9," my journal tends to take itself lightly, and it stays a little ambiguous.

I started my first journal in eighth grade. It was a small black book with gold glitter writing and a brass lock. I named it "Bubbles" and wrote to her every day.

— Geneen Roth, editor

Time

Jan. 13, 1970. It certainly feels like time to make some sort of journal entry.

— Maxine Kumin, poet

THE busy-ness of your day often excludes all but the crucial. Convince yourself, then, that journal keeping is crucial, absolutely worth a slot of time in the day. You set big and little priorities every day, placing things into two categories: "This must be done; that will be done if there's time." Every day, place your journal time in the first category. If you make a daily list of things to do, jot down "Journal" on that list. If you set aside time every day to read the paper or to walk the dog, then set aside a journal time, too.

The more fortification you build around your journal

time at the beginning, the more confident you'll become that it's worth protecting. The time you spend writing to God can be as soul-satisfying as going into a room to talk alone with a friend. Make it relaxing: bring a cup of coffee, put on some Bach, take off your shoes.

Try to write at about the same time every day, whenever you're least likely to be disturbed. For doctors with beepers and mothers of newborns, those undisturbed moments may be hard to find, and once found, almost impossible to schedule. But try. Think about Davy Crockett, who scribbled in his diary up to the last day of the Battle of the Alamo! This was his last entry:

> Mar. 5, 1836. Pop, pop, pop! Bom, bom, bom! throughout the day. No time for memorandums now. Go ahead! Liberty and independence forever!

Maybe your house resembles the Alamo, and you feel, like Davy Crockett, a bit besieged and pressed for time. If so, write for just five minutes at first. My friend Carol tells herself that even if she has no time in the day, she can always write one sentence in her journal. Once she writes that sentence, she can't help but write a few more. Getting to the journal can be as hard as getting out of bed for a glass of water, but after you overcome your own arguments, it's refreshing.

Not everything that cries the loudest is the most urgent thing.

— Gordon MacDonald
Ordering Your Private World

Place

1851. *I have little opportunity to record thought or feelings, for want of opportunity to think. I am always surrounded by a flock of noisy children, and my head resounds with their noise like an empty barrel.*

— Ellen Birdseye Wheaton, pioneer
Diary entry

SOME people think that a journal must be written in complete silence, away from civilization. But journals have been scribbled on battlefields, carved on scraps of soap in crowded prisons, and often jotted in the White House, always a busy place. My favorite story of writing under pressure is of a nineteenth-century mother (maybe it was Ellen Birdseye Wheaton, poor woman) who had so many children she didn't know where to write. Her toddlers were forever climbing on the table when she tried to write there, so she scribbled while standing at the fireplace mantel.

Of course, most of us find it easier to think, pray, and write elsewhere, away from the questions and demands of others. Most contemplatives, after all, prefer remote monasteries to Times Square. "Now come away by yourselves to a quiet place," Jesus urged his disciples. The Gospel of Mark explains, "For there were people coming and going incessantly so that they had not even time for meals." Sound familiar? Jesus often went away by himself to the hills to pray, to feel the peace of God again.

All that the writer Mary McCarthy needed to write, she said, was "a nice peaceful place with some good light." For you, that "peaceful place" might mean a tree-house, a beach cabin with no phone, or a book-filled office at the English department after hours.

Most of us can never find absolute peace and quiet. We will have to do our best to write among noises. Maybe what you need isn't pristine silence but a subdued hum. If you write in a café, for instance, the clink of coffee spoons and the general buzz of conversation might be just the right amount of noise to keep you occupied with your journal. Find a spot where you're welcome to stay as long as you want.

A clergyman once said to me that a railway compartment,
if one has it to himself, is an extremely good place to pray
in "because there is just the right amount of distraction."

— C. S. Lewis
Letters to Malcolm

Procrastination

Do I have the courage to write? I do everything to put it off. I am afraid to get close to it — afraid of what I might say.

> — Gail Godwin, writer
> Diary entry

So much stands in the way.

You could think of your journal as a wide open steeplechase, a country course covering hundreds of acres, where you are the rider and your pen is the horse. Together you jump stone walls and cross creeks. You accomplish parts of this course every day, just for the leap and plunge of it.

Wooden hurdles have been set up around the course. Each day you face different obstacles, otherwise known as Excuses for Not Writing. "I'm too tired" is the most arduous hurdle for some. Others find it hard to overcome the obstacles of "I keep forgetting," "Duty before journal," and "I'd rather be mucking stalls."

The best thing to do when presented with an obstacle is to jump and be done with it. Whenever you approach a hurdle, guide your horse to the center of the jump. Allow no wishy-washy wondering, or the horse will balk and shy away. Look straight over the horse's ears and go with her as she flies. If all goes as planned, the horse will come down on the other side with a thump and a light grunt — with your rump still in the saddle — and you both will go on.

Have a tenderness and determination toward your writing, a sense of humor and a deep patience that you are doing the right thing. Avoid getting caught by that small, gnawing mouse of doubt.

— Natalie Goldberg
Writing Down the Bones

Discipline

I am in a limbo that needs to be patterned from within.

— May Sarton
Journal of a Solitude

THE word *discipline* comes from *disciple*, which means "to take, accept, learn." Discipline is a term often confused with the words *dismaying, distasteful,* and *disgusting.* How is it that some people can run two miles every morning before breakfast, fix well-balanced dinners every night (lean meat, wheat bread, skim milk, two vegetables), and write three thank-you notes before falling into bed (with carefully turned-down sheets) at ten o'clock exactly? You know the answer: these people have discipline.

There's only one difference between those with

discipline and those without: when disciplined people are faced with a task they don't want to do, they do it anyway.

It's easy for anyone to *start* a journal. But the only way to *keep* a journal is to make a discipline out of it, to write every day, no matter what obstacles fall in the way. You ask me, do I write every day? Well, no . . . but almost. Daily is the ideal; it's much better to decide to write every day than every so often. If I miss one day, it becomes easy to miss the next one and the next. Then, of course, guilt creeps in, making it even harder for me to come back to writing. So I work hard at steering myself to my journal every night.

It seems that we all have the discipline to do whatever we feel is essential. If it's a round of golf every day for physical fitness, we'll find the stamina for it. If it's a book a month for mental fitness, we'll find the energy to stay up late to finish one book before the next one comes in the mail. If we could just keep a journal with the idea that it's a daily essential, we might find that it's not a burden after all. It's more like a home-cooked supper with dessert.

But slow down. Remember the root meanings of discipline: "take," "accept," and "learn." These are passive words that indicate receptivity to another's action. Mary of Bethany sat at Jesus' feet, learning from him, while Martha bustled through her last-minute hostess preparations, not listening. In that story it was Mary who was the disciple, the disciplined person. Mary took the time to sit down and listen.

Just you give Mary a little chance as well as Martha.

> — C. S. Lewis
> *Letters to an American Lady*

At this instant

December 10, 1843. Father read to us in dear "Pilgrim's Progress." In the eve father and mother and Anna and I had a long talk. I was very unhappy, and we all cried. Anna and I cried in bed, and I prayed God to keep us all together.

— Louisa May Alcott
Diary entry

WHEN you keep a journal, you are taking notes on life as it is happening. "Autobiography is 'what I remember,'" wrote May Sarton, "whereas a journal has to do with 'what I am now, at this instant.'" Though Louisa May Alcott's *Little Women* is based on her childhood, the tone of her book is much cheerier — less believable, actually — than the tone of the diary she kept when she was eleven. A journal records the ongoing discovery, if you can be heartbreakingly honest, of your inside self. One stanza of a song called "Hey, Jesus," sung by the Indigo Girls, is rippingly honest:

> I don't really think it's fair.
> You've got the power to make a soul believe in you.
> Then we call you in our despair,
> and you don't come through.

At times you will be frustrated with God, or he will be frustrated with you. Your relationship, though one of love, is also one of struggle.

Don't be afraid to tell the truth. If you hesitate to write honestly because you're afraid your journal will be discovered, then be creative about keeping it absolutely private. Lock your journal in a strongbox and hide it under your bed. Write your entries in the form of ambiguous poetry. Write in code, or just scribble unintelligibly. Let your journal be a place to paint a true picture, not a place to whitewash.

Notice how honestly the Psalmists sang to God in both their grief and their high joy:

> For I eat ashes like bread, and mingle tears with my drink, because of thy indignation and anger; for thou hast taken me up and thrown me away.

> Psalm 102:9-10 (RSV)

Sing to God, sing praise to his name, extol him who rides on the clouds. . . . God sets the lonely in families, he leads forth the prisoners with singing.

Psalm 68:4, 6 (NIV)

Like the Psalmists, we can afford to be honest with God.

I feel caved in like Daniel today, but for different, less spectacular reasons. I've been complaining here in the journal, but it's the way I feel after a tussle, fitting thirty-three pounds of boy into a squirming pajama sleeper.

— FRONT

He knows us

*April 4, 1947. Good Friday. Had a pious thought, but I
am not going to write it down. The best place to hide,
this afternoon, was in church. It rained hard and you
could hear the rain beating all over the long roof.*

— Thomas Merton
Diary entry

IF you're finding it hard to write Significant Thoughts
in your journal, maybe you're being too hard on yourself. Whatever you want to write is important! God is
interested in anything you want to tell him. He's never
shocked by what you might say, because he knows you.
It's all right; it is *all right*. You can write imaginative or
technical words, purposeful or playful sentences, on any

subject you can think of. Just tell him the truth; he knows it already, and he wants you to know it, too.

If you need to loosen up, try writing as fast as the pen allows. Don't worry about how it sounds. Don't worry about the number of grammatical errors you may have committed. This is the time to write, not to criticize yourself. Don't even look back at your entry until you've finished.

At the same time, though, think what you mean to say. Shun clichés, because clichés avoid thoughts that should be expressed plainly. Even as you're writing quickly and almost carelessly in your journal, keep an ear tuned for repetitive sayings like "heavy burden," and watch out for those say-nothing expressions like "personal growth experience." Before you write down a phrase you've heard from someone else, think about what you want to say yourself.

When you do put down your pen and reread your passage, resist the urge to edit. This is private, honest writing, and what you've written is good for the journal. Let it stand. In my home I used to tutor a first-grader in art. Allison and I never erased anything in our drawings. We called this "being brave." Instead of erasing, we incorporated the stray pencil mark into the drawing, making it a cloud or a flock of birds far away. Be brave. Write whatever comes to mind or heart, and leave it there on paper.

But be patient, too, with yourself. It takes a long
time to unwrap those protective layers covering the heart.

I realize very little of my interior is showing as yet in
this journal. I am too much living a life of mother and
wife now to unfold. It is all . . . in the pleats.

— Maxine Kumin

Pressing out

August 6, 1849. I think spelling is very funny, I spelt infancy infantsy, and they said it was wrong, but I don't see why, because if my seven little cousins died when they were infants, they must have died in their infantsy; but infancy makes it seem as if they hadn't really died but we just made believe.

— Catherine Elizabeth Havens, age 11
Diary entry

WRITING in your journal is a way of expressing, "pressing out." You press out your emotions and thoughts like cooked apples through a sieve.

Sometimes this act of expression is forced and painful, but at other times the writing itself is a release from

pressure. My friend Rae Marie once told me that when
she doesn't write, her whole day is cockeyed. "Sometimes
I don't know what's wrong," she said, "but I just feel
uneasy all day. Then I write something in my journal
and can spill out what I'm feeling and find out what I'm
thinking."

In the introduction to a volume of her journal
entries and letters called *Locked Rooms and Open Doors,*
Anne Morrow Lindbergh wrote,

> The habit of writing almost daily in my diary probably
> saved my sanity. If I could write out moods which could
> be admitted to no one, they became more manageable, as
> though neatly stacked on a high shelf.

And the writer Louise Bogan in her journal wrote, simply,

> I put all this down in order to clarify my own heart.

Expression is not all dark and serious, of course. In
making the world, God expressed himself by fashioning
the peacock with its wild, royal train of plumes and a
crest like a diamond tiara. He invented the baby penguin
that peeks out from its father's legs. And in his inexpli-
cable wisdom God "pressed out" the happy, nonstop
chatterbox, the mockingbird.

I write in order to attain that feeling of tension relieved and function achieved which a cow enjoys on giving milk.

— H. L. Mencken, journalist

Why negative is normal

No one ever talks about their feelings, anyway,
without dressing them in dreams and laughter.
I guess it's just too painful, otherwise.

— Jackson Browne, songwriter

MOST people don't like to dwell on what ails them. They shake their heads at journal keepers, who seem to *need* to keep written records of their rotting marriages or their unnameable depressions. If you just don't think about it, people say, the sadness will go away eventually. But if you dwell on it, the bad feeling will hang around like an alley cat fed by a sympathetic fool.

Does your journal sound mostly negative? "Why has my motley diary no jokes?" asked Emerson in his journal. "Because it is a soliloquy, and every man is grave alone."

Writing sad, serious words in one's journal is normal, but it might be good to discover why negative is normal.

Being alone with God in your journal means that you can say exactly how you are and who you are. There is no one else around, no one to pretend to. You are "stripped to the infant gaze," as May Sarton describes the feeling of being in the presence of angels.

"One would like to present," Anne Morrow Lindbergh said about journal writing, "truthfully and not glamorized, what happened. This is what life is, one feels; these are the conditions, the terms on which one accepts or rejects it — and one loses too much in the rejection."

Writing in prayer about the most sensitive aspects of our lives will of course cause in us a serious attitude. We couldn't expect to be jolly when confronted with our inner nature. It makes us sad to remember certain things from our past — difficult times with a lover, a friend whom we let down. God brings them to mind again when we write in our journals.

Don't be afraid to be negative. God won't walk away in a huff. Put it all down on paper, the whole truth as it looks to you today. Tomorrow you can write again, and God will still be there, listening.

Write your heart out.

— Bernard Malamud, novelist

Risk

*Somehow the need to be genuine, even at the risk of
being taken advantage of, compels me to reveal.*

— Tess Gallagher, poet

THE word *risk* comes from a Latin root meaning
"danger at sea," "rock," "that which cuts." It sounds
as though sailors faced a row of risks when they came too
close to shore. What is it that you as a journal keeper
risk? One thing you risk is a growth in awareness of yourself in relation with God, and that can cut.

Before you started writing your journal, you might
not have had to face your hidden self. Now as you write,
you try to tell how you genuinely feel, and your hidden
self sometimes cries out, "Lousy!" Wouldn't it be better
not to have to face that inner self every day? The writer

Flannery O'Connor didn't think so. She wrote to a Catholic priest, "I wish we would hear more preaching about the harm we do from the things we do not face."

What is risky about keeping a journal is that you open up more and more of yourself as you keep writing, as though your soul were a well-wrapped gift from God. After you break through the packing material and wrapping paper bound with strings, ribbons, and tape, there's a box. Inside the box is tissue, surrounding a small black case. Inside the case is a mirror.

The mirror reflects an image of your soul, literally your "true self." It's disturbing to see yourself so clearly. What if you don't like seeing the real you, after all the trouble of unwrapping? Well, you could close up the gift and put it away in the tissue, the box, and the packing material again. But you would never be able to forget the face you saw in that mirror, all your invisible loves and struggles made plain. "It is the invisible that God sees," Flannery O'Connor said, "and that the Christian must look for."

The contemplative Julian of Norwich wrote, "No created being can comprehend how much, and how sweetly, and how tenderly our maker loves us." When we find ourselves looking at our true selves, we may not like what we see. But God sees us as we are and loves us. This is no blind love — the God who says "yes" is also the God who can sternly say "no." But all he offers us he offers us in love.

When you write in your journal, you risk getting emotional, because emotions rise to the surface of your words. You risk feeling angry and defeated. You also "risk" feeling wonderful, because the world is full of wonder. You risk laughing out loud in a quiet café, because you might get the feeling sometimes that God is grinning at you in love.

The greatest hazard to life is to risk nothing. The person who risks nothing does nothing, has nothing, is nothing. He may avoid suffering and sorrow, but he simply cannot learn, feel, change, grow, love — live.

— Rod Brownfield, writer

Find a comrade

But it's painful to journey this way, like a moon or a moth
Going around and around some dangerous thing.

— Barbara L. Greenberg, poet

WHO can soothe the ache that comes when you write your heart out? Sometimes, no matter how long you listen for his voice, God seems far away and silent. This distance can wound; communion with God is not always marked by closeness and joy, as the Psalmist reminds us:

> I, O Lord, cry to thee;
>   in the morning my prayer comes before thee.
> O Lord, why dost thou cast me off?
>   Why dost thou hide thy face from me?
>
> (Ps. 88:13-14, RSV)

When you feel that God is far away, find a comrade. Reading a journal entry aloud to someone can dissipate the pain.

Whenever I teach journal workshops, I include a time of journal writing, then a time of "readback and feedback." It's scary to read one's raw impressions to others. People risk becoming emotional over their own words, and they risk getting weird stares from the group. The most common response to an intimate entry, though, isn't shock but recognition: "I thought no one else felt that way."

I wish I could hear you read from your journal. Then I'm sure I could say, "Yes, you have it there! You're telling the truth. Don't be afraid to write more. Dig deeper."

But since I can't hear you read, you may want to find someone who will listen thoughtfully to your writings, a friend who will keep your secrets absolutely undercover and won't try to critique your journal entries as though they were *contest* entries for a writing competition. For your part, you can give this friend reciprocal support: a listening ear and a compassionate heart.

When you find someone who finds value in your words and nudges you to keep writing, someone you in turn can encourage, then you've found a comrade. *Comrade* comes from Old French, meaning literally, "soldier sharing the same room." As a friend of mine said once, "What are comrades but friends under fire?"

We walk through so many myths of each other and ourselves; we are so thankful when someone sees us for who we are and accepts us.

— Natalie Goldberg
Writing Down the Bones

Balance

Blue skies all week, indigo, with little fog banks setting off
mauve sunsets.
                                                    — FRONT

THERE'S nothing wrong with a negative-sounding
journal, unless it makes you too depressed to write
in it. If you feel your journal is too dark, too weighty, too
Germanic, then balance that voice of negativity in your
journal. Take a vacation from brooding. Go Caribbean.

- Glue some photographs or postcards in the journal. Slip
  in encouraging notes from friends and relations.
- Make a heading on the page like "Bright Spots" and list
  the good moments of the day, the small acts that go
  unnoticed. In Oregon, I wrote down this "Bright Spot":

Eric prayed, "Thanks for this food and this night. Thanks for taking a bath and getting wrinkles." All this while lying in bed, twirling my hair and sucking his thumb.

- Write a limerick or a parable in your journal. Record the dialogue of the two preschoolers you heard today. Try writing a fairy tale, or put on paper the score of that great tune you've been humming.
- Doodle. Draw a cartoon, or sketch the scene from your window. Press in a tulip petal or a soup-can label.
- Take your journal for a walk. When you find a new vantage point, write from there.
- Quote a lot. Whatever you think sounds interesting at the time, from whatever source, write it down. "Perhaps all the dragons in our lives," wrote the German poet Rainer Maria Rilke, "are only princesses waiting to see us once beautiful and brave."

All this reminds me of something I heard about Hopi Indians. They say that to be a useful Hopi is to be one who has a quiet heart and takes part in all the dances. Yes.

— Robert Fulghum, writer

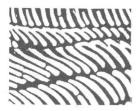

Watchkeeping

Prayer

He wants nothing better than that you should listen to him.

— Anonymous
The Cloud of Unknowing

WHEN we pray, we can't see the one we're talking with. But on the journal page we can see the effects of God, who *wants* to talk with us, who actually enjoys weaving himself through our day's routine. "Call to me," said the Lord in the book of Jeremiah, "and I will answer you, and will tell you great and hidden things which you have not known."

By addressing each day's journal entry to God, we call, asking him to answer us. And the astounding thing is, he does answer. In journal keeping of this kind, we never write alone in a vacuum. We write in relationship, in love, with God.

He wants utter communication with us. Is it silly to think that God could speak to our hearts today as well as in the words we hear in church? There is *something* new under the sun: God's words of love for us. As the prophet Jeremiah wrote in the book of Lamentations, "You came near when I called you, and you said, 'Do not fear.'" In *Listening to the God Who Speaks,* theologian Klaus Bockmuehl wrote, "He still speaks today, turning each moment into one of grace."

In the poem "Summer Grass" Carl Sandburg wrote what could be an analogy of a journal keeper who writes a wrenching prayer, and God, who answers in kindness:

Summer grass aches and whispers.

It wants something;
it calls and sings;
it pours out wishes to the overhead stars.

The rain hears;
the rain answers;
the rain is slow coming;
the rain wets the face of the grass.

My heart has heard you say, "Come and talk with me, O my people." And my heart responds, "Lord, I am coming."

— Psalm 27:8 (Living Bible)

Practice the presence

In Adult Sunday School this morning we were discussing the quiet classic, The Practice of the Presence of God. *The pastor asked, "What does it mean to 'practice the presence of God'?" To depend on him daily in everything, we decided. Simple, eh? Hardly. But in trying to practice that this week, I've begun to ask God, "What do you want me to do today? What should I say to my friend when I see her? Where's that missing shoe?" And he cares — he wants a back and forth dialogue, a constant intimacy like that. It involves listening, which grows easier — listening, and hearing — with the practice of the presence of God.*

— FRONT

PRACTICING God's presence is the act of remembering him. When you walk along a beach or lakeshore, remind yourself that God is thinking about you in love. "As you hear the wind, and feel it too," said evangelist John Wesley, "you will know you are under the guidance of God's Spirit . . . namely by feeling it in your soul." You may be having supper with your friend at a restaurant or talking with a kind stranger on a train when you remember and say in your heart, "God is with us, right here."

"Yes," God might reply in his quiet way. "I AM."

Everyone is able to have these familiar conversations with God. Some more, some less — He knows our capabilities. Let us make a start. Perhaps He only waits for us to make one whole-hearted resolve.

— Brother Lawrence
The Practice of the Presence of God

A gentle silence

And behold, the Lord passed by, and a great and strong wind rent the mountains, and broke in pieces the rocks before the Lord, but the Lord was not in the wind; and after the wind an earthquake, but the Lord was not in the earthquake; and after the earthquake a fire, but the Lord was not in the fire; and after the fire a still small voice.

— 1 Kings 19:11-12 (RSV)

WHAT does it mean to hear God? When you stop writing in your journal to listen, are you waiting for an audible voice?

The great prophet Elijah hid in a cave, pouting. But he waited for God to speak to him. To such a sad prophet, God chose not to speak in a stormy, earthquaking, or fiery voice. God spoke in a still, small voice, which translated literally from the Hebrew means "the sound of a gentle silence." Mother Teresa of Calcutta said, "We need to find God, and he cannot be found in noise and restlessness. God is the friend of silence."

That still, small voice is quieter than the sound of creation waiting for spring. The English mystic Julian of Norwich wrote, "God is the still point at the center." But since it is so quiet, even the journal keeper who prays to hear God's voice might miss it.

In one of George Bernard Shaw's plays, *Back to Methuselah,* the character Adam talks about God speaking to him. "To me there is only one voice. It is very low; but it is so near that it is like a whisper from within myself. There is no mistaking it for any voice of the birds or beasts."

When God told Solomon he would give him whatever he wanted, Solomon asked for wisdom, which means literally "a hearing heart." Solomon knew that with a heart attuned to God's voice, he could make decisions and write proverbs with God's counsel. God was so pleased with this request that he also gave Solomon gold, honor, and the gift of poetry. A hearing heart, God said, was the best thing Solomon could have asked for.

I remember reading in the Bible as a grade schooler that I should pray in my closet and not pray loudly on street corners as the Pharisees did. So for months when I came home from school, I went into my walk-in closet and prayed, waiting for God to answer. I stayed as still as a rabbit; I stretched my ears toward God to hear him speaking. I wasn't sure what I was listening for, but I felt that I would recognize him when he spoke. Maybe it was the silence that was too loud. I think I was hoping either for a little magic or for a great prophecy to tell the nations, but I never heard him until years later. I never dreamed that he would speak inside me, kind and full of love. How could I know that the Holy Spirit's voice would be just like the voice of Jesus?

> I have said this while I am still with you. But the one who is coming to stand by you, the Holy Spirit whom the Father will send in my name, will be your teacher and will bring to your minds all that I have said to you.
>
> — John 14:25-26 (Phillips)

An NBC News correspondent once interviewed an autistic girl. The girl would not speak, but she communicated with others by writing on her computer monitor. "I hear God's finest whispers," she wrote. Taken aback, the correspondent asked, "And what does God say to you?" The girl answered by typing, "He says he loves me, too."

What are you going to do, and how are you going to lay hold on him?

> — Anonymous
> *The Cloud of Unknowing*

The mind and heart

Eli perceived that the Lord was calling the boy. Therefore Eli said to Samuel, "Go, lie down; and if he calls you, you shall say, 'Speak, Lord, for thy servant hears.'"

— 1 Samuel 3:8-9 (RSV)

GOD wants to talk with us — he wants to talk *with* us, not just listen to us. In the book of Hosea he said, "It is I who answer and look after you."

Listening has always been a hallmark of the saints. One of the Psalmists wrote, "I will listen to what God the Lord will say; he promises peace to his people, his saints." The contemplative St. Teresa of Ávila advised her readers to "listen attentively to whatever our Lord shall speak to us interiorly." The mind, she said, should rest, but "love is still to be kept awake."

Not that the mind is evil, or that it should fall into a coma when we listen to God, but sometimes it should rest. Take a break from worrying and calculating. The head seems to work too hard at times like these. Our minds often want something tangible or audible from God when all he wants is for our hearts, not just our mouths, to be quiet enough to hear him. This is faith hard at work.

I have learned . . . that the head does not hear anything until the heart has listened, and what the heart knows today the head will understand tomorrow.

— James Stephens, writer

Hearing a voice

Your voice falls on me as they say love should, like an enormous yes.

— Philip Levine, poet

I REMEMBER I was maneuvering the vacuum cleaner around the living room with two preschoolers and a dog underfoot when I asked God out of desperation, "What do you want me to *do?*" It was one of those life essay questions; I didn't expect an answer. "Listen," was his answer. "Listen." The first time I could hear him was under the noise of the vacuum.

We may not always hear God speaking when we pray. Most often God responds in plain, unspoken ways: in the smile of an old friend, in a fitting Bible verse that we "happen" to come across three times in one day. Sometimes we come to an understanding of God's response simply by staying open to clues he may hide for us in the world. We can almost guess God's response to a question of ours when a shaft of sun breaks out of dark clouds and lights up the sea.

But learning to hear God's voice, like learning to do anything else, is a process. It may be that you *have* heard God and not realized it. At first it's just a word or phrase you may hear inside, like "Yes" or "Sit down and wait." It's like hearing someone whispering in another room — God's voice is that quiet. Later, he may give you personal, specific assurances, using names and responding intimately to your questions. What you hear resembles God's voice in the Bible, because it *is* the same voice, speaking to you now.

How do you know this isn't just your conscience speaking? Because this is a different voice from your own. This voice is wiser, more accepting of your faults than you are, and is able to surprise you. Often I ask in my journal, "Lord, do you mean this?" and he responds, "Yes; and I mean *this*," as if he were drawing a wide circle around my thoughts.

Sometimes he uses words whose literal meaning makes all the difference in understanding. Once I asked what I should do for two friends who seemed, in a sense, to be falling. "Succor" was his answer. In the dictionary I found the literal meaning of *succor:* "to run under (someone who is falling)."

How do you know this is not an evil voice trying to deceive you? Julian of Norwich said that the devil produces only counterfeit speech, accusatory and not loving. Jesus said that those who know God recognize his voice, and by knowing his voice they can recognize the wrong voice. In 1760 John Wesley wrote in his diary about a woman who came to him

as she said, with a message from the Lord, to tell me, I was laying up treasures on earth, taking my ease, and minding only my eating and drinking. I told her, God knew me better; and if He had sent her, He would have sent her with a more proper message.

I do a lot of listening. Prayer, as you know, is not meant to be a monologue but a dialogue. It is communion, a friendly talk.

— Samuel Logan Brengle,
Salvation Army Commissioner

Write it down

I sit down alone, only God is here.

— John Wesley

WHAT do you do if, after writing in your journal, you listen and think you hear something? Write it down. Don't worry if you're not sure where the words came from. It's the most common thing in the world to think, "No, God didn't speak to me just then. It was the wind. It was my mind making something up." Let the doubts come and go, but continue to write in your journal, which is a form of prayer, and keep listening.

Centuries ago, Julian of Norwich heard God speak to her and wrote down the words:

So he says this, "Pray inwardly, even though you find no joy in it. For it does good, though you feel nothing, see nothing, yes, even though you think you cannot pray. For when you are dry and empty, sick and weak, your prayers please me, though there is little enough to please you. All believing prayer is precious to me."

In the spring of 1991 I was traveling through Great Britain and Ireland with my friend Luci Shaw, who is a poet and a photographer. We were following the wonderful roundabout path of the nineteenth-century poet Gerard Manley Hopkins for *A Holy Struggle,* my book of sonnets based on his life. One night at a bed and breakfast south of Dublin, I sat on the bed writing in my journal:

> Everyone has been very kind, giving directions to us all day, as I've heard they'll do till the sun goos down an' the cows come hoom. We're in among the cows now — I can smell them outside. We've just had tea in the "lounge," which is their living room. Tea was served as usual on a tray with biscuits, sugar and cream. Very warm hospitality. Lord, what do you say?

He answered:

> I say I love you, and I give you these things as gifts. Take them in remembrance of me. Yes! They are sacraments for

your health, for your soul's nourishment. I love you and I keep you forever in my heart. Yes. This much is true: I hold you as a child holds a fawn. All those things you have searched for I have given you. Do not neglect your loves. They are still and always with you. Pray for them as they pray for you, constantly and always. Amen. I love you.

I'm convinced that hearing is not a spiritual gift that comes only to a few chosen ones. The more I talk with others about their own journal-keeping habits, the more I hear them say, "Oh yes, definitely, God answers back."

But if you don't hear God speaking inwardly to you, don't worry that there must be something wrong with you. God not only speaks but shows. He reveals bits of his character to us in every created thing. Consider how God is like smoke, like birdsong, like a blue whale. Think of the times he sends you a friend who speaks just the right words to you, or the way he points out magazine articles that spark ideas for your work. Oh yes, definitely, God answers back.

Journal keeping serves as a wonderful tool for withdrawing and communing with the Father. When I write, it is as if I am in direct conversation with Him.

— Gordon MacDonald
Ordering Your Private World

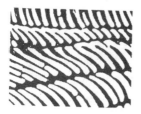

Sea Journey

Look back now

I always forget how important the empty days are.

— May Sarton

BY writing a paragraph or two in this book or in your own journal every day, you are, either consciously or unconsciously, making an account of your spiritual life. You are telling God your life story as it goes on. Your journal is a record of days — some very hard, some almost easy — which, strung together in a notebook, make a certain amount of sense. From your life story you could pick out plot lines, main characters, and even an informing metaphor or two. All this comes from writing something truthful every day.

Vincent Van Gogh wrote to his brother Theo,

It is the experience and hard work of every day which alone will ripen in the long run and will allow one to do something truer and more complete. . . .

The more you write, the easier it will become to say what you want to say. The easier that becomes, the more you will want to keep writing.

Turn back to the first page of your journal and read what you've written so far. Here it's written in black and white, or in various colors. You can refer to it later, days or even years from now. You can find connecting threads that you never noticed at the time you wrote. As St. Paul told the Corinthians, "You can look back now and see how the hand of God was in that sorrow," that good retreat, that last year of a friend's life, that slow time when nothing seemed to be happening.

We do not know today whether we are busy or idle. In times when we thought ourselves indolent, we have afterwards discovered that much was accomplished and much was begun in us.

— Ralph Waldo Emerson

A pattern

Suppose a peddler came to the door
to sell you the story of your life.
It was one of many he had in a bag;
but this one was yours.

— Sheila Nickerson
"On the Origin of Stories"

WRITING the story of your life in a journal, even over the course of just a few weeks, reveals a pattern, just as weaving a few inches of yarn on a loom reveals one. At first the materials look tangled. But soon the pattern appears, one you weren't quite expecting. It seems just right, now that you see it displayed before you: rosepath, bird's-eye twill, or monk's belt, instead of rows and rows of plain old tabby weave.

After you write for a few years, you can chart the times of activity and stillness, like rings in a tree.

If you look back over entries every few months or so, you can make illuminating short-term discoveries: a small crisis is resolved; a prayer is answered; pain and joy move in quick cycles.

If you look back at your entries over the years, you will see growth — perhaps in insight or in the ability to nurture others. And you may experience some self-revelations: you may find an untapped artistic gift, an unexplored but deeply felt emotion, a surprising source of contentment.

You will also find patterns and rhythms through your journal; you will see Frederick Buechner's assertion — that God's purpose is working itself out in our lives — in action. You will see God's shaping hand in decisions made and paths taken, in times of turbulence and still-ness.

You will see the repeated motifs of your own life — not just a life pattern but a pattern of the heart.

King David was a passionate person all of his life, exuberant in poetry and song, in love and battle. Throughout his life, his passion for God deepened and matured. God kept to the basic pattern he had begun weaving in the shepherd boy: joy, struggle, pain, peace; joy, struggle, pain, peace.

Reading Ved Mehta's article in The New Yorker *on circumstances leading to his American education, it was easy to see what he called coincidences fitting into a pattern. "Looking back now," he said, "it seems inevitable, but then it always does."*

— FRONT

The parable of the pitcher

Nov. 25, 1881. I ought to endeavour to keep, to a certain extent, a record of passing impressions, of all that comes, that I see, and feel, and observe. To catch and keep something of life — that's what I mean.

— Henry James, writer

AN empty pitcher stands by the door, not knowing what to do. Suddenly a man comes past the door and stops by the pitcher. "Hello, little one," he says. "What are you doing there? Why are you not pouring milk?"

"Because," says the pitcher, "I have no one to pour me. And I have no milk."

"No milk!" says the man. "Why, I have a cow and no pitcher — what do you think of that?"

And so they go off together, man and pitcher, gladly, for now each has the other.

Think of the pitcher as a journal book that sits off by itself in the bookstore, waiting to be used. It waits there until one day a journal keeper without a journal comes along, takes it home, and pours fresh words into it. A journal can never be used for its created purpose until a journal keeper takes it home and writes in it.

Then you shall call, and the Lord will answer; you shall cry, and he will say, Here I am.

— Isaiah 58:9 (RSV)

248.46
SM655

LINCOLN CHRISTIAN COLLEGE AND SEMINARY   89374

248.46 SM655   89374
Smith, Margaret D., 1958-
Journal keeper

DEMCO